MW01256448

DEAN'S CUISINES

67 RECIPES COMMEMORATING 67 YEARS

FRED BROOKS JR.

Even,
Pleasure to meet you Brother!

[signature]

Self -n- DAYS
Publish 30
This Is The Year For
Your New Book

@fredbrooksjr
the realtor.

W W W . S E L F P U B L I S H N 3 0 D A Y S . C O M

Published by Self Publish -N- 30 Days

Printed in the United States of America

ISBN: 978-1703672695 1. Cookbook 2. Southern Cuisines DEAN'S CUISINES: 67 RECIPES COMMEMORATING 67 YEARS

Disclaimer/Warning:
This book is intended for cooking and informative purposes only. The author or publisher do not guarantee that anyone will be successful in creating cuisines. The author and publisher shall have neither liability responsibility to anyone with respect to any loss or damage cause, or alleged to be caused, directly or indirectly by the information contained in this book.

In Loving Memory of My Mother
Mrs. Geraldine "Dean" Williams Brooks
Sunrise March 20, 1951 – Sunset December 13, 2018

"Mom, you are truly missed. You touched the lives of so many people and had a special way of bringing out the best in everyone. Additionally, I am thankful for all the sacrifices you made to ensure that we had everything we needed through the years. You will always live on in our hearts."

Your Son, Fred Brooks Jr. & Your Loving Family

ABOUT MRS. GERALDINE WILLIAMS BROOKS

Geraldine Williams Brooks, lovingly known as "Dean," was born on March 20, 1951 in New Orleans, Louisiana. She was the tenth of twelve children born to Mattie Cummings Williams and the late Henry Williams Sr. Dean never knew a stranger because she always made everyone feel at home. She was selfless in everything that she did and was always willing to lend a helping hand to anyone who crossed her path. She had a heart of gold and her generosity was immeasurable. She gave so much and was loved by so many.

Dean was united in holy matrimony to Fredrick Brooks, Sr., and to this union two children were born, Fredrick Jr. and Tonika. She labored tirelessly to raise her children and took special joy in caring for her only grandson, Tre'Vyon (TJ), who was her heart and soul. She spoiled her nieces and nephews as if they were her own children. Her absence leaves a hole in the hearts and lives of all who knew her, and she is greatly missed.

She also showed her love to her family through her cooking. If anyone in the family so much as mentioned that they wanted a certain dish, within days Dean was knocking at your door with the dish in hand, or calling you to come and pick up your dish.

As her niece and the mother of her goddaughter, her cooking made a tremendous impact upon our lives. My favorite dishes that she cooked for me were her flautas and her German chocolate cake. I did not like coconut but after eating her coconut icing on the German chocolate cake, I became a lover of coconut.

Dean was the daytime caretaker of my daughter, her goddaughter, while I worked until my daughter began school. My daughter loved Dean's rice and gravy and would not eat anyone else's gravy because it did not taste like Dean's gravy.

I will truly miss her delicious dishes and her loving smile.

Latricia Ford-Anderson

TABLE OF CONTENTS

Shrimp Fettuccine 1

Shrimp, Sausage, and Chicken
    Jambalaya 3

Seafood Gumbo 5

Flautas. 7

Chicken Tetrazzini. 9

Crawfish Stew 11

Ribs, Ribs, Ribs 13

Southern Buttermilk Biscuits 16

Skillet Cornbread. 18

Simple & Delicious Holiday Yams . .20

Creamy Macaroni & Cheese 22

Chicken Pot Pie 25

Cajun Blast Pork Roast 27

Baked Beans 30

Cajun BBQ Cocktail Meatballs 32

Waffle Omelet. 34

The Best Punch 36

Excellent Stuffed Peppers 38

Deviled Eggs 41

Spaghetti with Crawfish and Red
    Sauce 43

Red Beans and Rice. 45

Juicy Seasoned Burgers 47

Southern Cornbread Dressing 49

Rice Dressing 52

Beef Stroganoff. 54

Oysters and Angel Hair Pasta 56

Baked Grits and Greens with Bacon 58

Crackling Cornbread. 60

"Panama Limited" French Toast. . . . 62

Baked Cushaw. 64

Chicken Spaghetti 66

Mighty Good Meat Loaf. 68

Shrimp Stuffed Eggplant 70

Pork Chop Casserole. 72

Chicken and Dumplings. 74

New Orleans Fried Catfish. 77

Louisiana Crawfish Ravioli with
    Crawfish Cream Sauce. 80

Cheesy Potatoes with Smoked
    Sausage .83

Smoked Chili Lime Turkey Wings. . 85

Rice & Gravy Steaks 87

Authentic Louisiana Crawfish Boil. .90

Slow Cooker Crawfish & Crab Dip. .93

Slow Cooker Spicy Chicken Wings in Barbecue Sauce 95

Cajun Chicken and Fried Rice 97

The Sweet Stuff!

Cajun Blackberry Dumplings 103

7Up® Pound Cake 106

Preserved Figs 108

Vanilla Custard Ice Cream 111

Lemon Pound Cake 113

Slow Cooker Peach Cobbler 115

Sour Cream Cake 117

Tea Cakes 119

Raisin Bread Pudding 121

Rum Sauce 123

Peanut Butter Cookies 125

Creamy No Bake Banana Pudding . 127

Traditional Banana Pudding 129

Italian Cream Cake 131

New Orleans Beignets 133

Geraldine's Pecan Pralines 135

Quick Sweet Potato Pie 137

Old Fashioned Sugar Cookies 139

Classic Pecan Pie 141

Blueberry Gateau 143

Slow Cooker Apple Pie 146

German Sweet Chocolate Cake . . . 148

Gingerbread 151

Old Fashioned Pineapple Upside Down Cake 153

═══ 1951 ═══
SHRIMP FETTUCCINE

SERVES 8

Directions

1. Melt butter in medium saucepan. Add onion and bell pepper and cook until tender. Stir in flour and cover. Cook 15 minutes, stirring often. Add parsley, garlic, cayenne, and salt. Cook 5 minutes.

2. Add half and half, Velveeta®, and shrimp. Cook on low heat for 20 minutes.

3. Cook fettuccine as directed on the package and drain. Toss shrimp mixture and fettuccine together and pour into a 1½- to 2-quart baking dish. Sprinkle with parmesan cheese and bake at 350 degrees for 15 to 20 minutes. Garnish with parsley and serve.

Note: Crawfish can be substituted for shrimp.

SOURCE: MRS. GERALDINE WILLIAMS BROOKS

1 stick butter

1 bell pepper, chopped

2 tablespoons parsley, minced

¼ teaspoon cayenne pepper

1 pint half and half

1 pound peeled and deveined shrimp

½ cup grated parmesan cheese

1 onion, chopped

3 tablespoons flour

1 clove garlic, minced

1 teaspoon salt

½ pound Velveeta® cheese

1 pound fettuccine pasta

$=$ CHEF NOTES $=$

_____

_____

_____

_____

_____

_____

_____

_____

_____

_____

_____

_____

_____

_____

_____

_____

_____

_____

_____

_____

_____

_____

SHRIMP, SAUSAGE, AND CHICKEN JAMBALAYA

SERVES 15

Directions

1. In a large pot, cover chicken with water and boil until tender, about 1 hour. Reserve stock. Discard skin and bones. Cut meat into small pieces and set aside.

2. In a heavy 4-quart pot, sauté sausage; remove with slotted spoon and drain on paper towels. Pour off drippings, add oil to pot and sauté green pepper, parsley, celery and onions 5 minutes.

3. Chop tomatoes and reserve liquid. Add tomatoes with liquid, broth and green onions. Stir in tomato paste, spices, and seasonings. Stir in rice. Add sausage and chicken.

4. Cover and cook 30 to 45 minutes over low heat, stirring occasionally. After most of the liquid has been absorbed by the rice, add shrimp. Cook until shrimp are pink (5 to 10 minutes).

SOURCE UNKNOWN1 (3-POUND) CHICKEN FRYER

3 cloves garlic, minced

1 cup chopped celery

2 (16-ounce) cans tomatoes

1 cup chopped green onions

1½ teaspoon thyme

2 teaspoons oregano

1 teaspoon salt

1 teaspoon black pepper

2 cups long grain rice

3 pounds raw shrimp, peeled, deveined, and rinsed (3X)

2 tablespoons olive oil

2 ¾ cup chopped fresh parsley

1 cup chopped onions

2 cups chicken broth

1 (6-ounce) can tomato paste

2 bay leaves

1 teaspoon chili powder

½ teaspoon cayenne pepper

1 teaspoon garlic powder

⅔ cup chopped green pepper

1 pound hot, smoked sausage, thinly sliced

= CHEF NOTES =

_____

_____

_____

_____

_____

_____

_____

_____

_____

_____

_____

_____

_____

_____

_____

_____

_____

_____

_____

_____

_____

_____

═══ 1953 ═══
SEAFOOD GUMBO

SERVES 10

Directions

1. Fry okra in 6 tablespoon of oil over medium heat for 35 minutes. Set aside. Make roux by whisking bacon drippings and flour in large skillet. Cook slowly and watch carefully so that it doesn't burn, until it reaches a dark caramel color.

2. Stir in the chopped onions, bell pepper, garlic, celery, green onion and parsley. Cook until softened. Add sliced andouille sausage and cook 15 minutes on low; stirring constantly. Add crushed tomatoes.

3. In a large pot, boil water with shrimp peelings to make a stock. Discard peelings and add the roux mixture to the stock slowly. Stir in the okra and the rest of the seasonings. Simmer on low for about 2 hours. Stir in the crab meat and shrimp. Simmer for 15 minutes.

SOURCE: MRS. GERALDINE WILLIAMS BROOKS

1½ pounds fresh okra

8 to 10 cups water

1 large can whole tomatoes, crushed

4 cloves garlic, chopped

3 ribs celery, chopped

1 bunch green onions, chopped

¾ cup parsley, chopped fine

1 pound andouille sausage, sliced

8 tablespoons bacon drippings

6 tablespoons oil

8 tablespoons flour

2 large onions, chopped

2 tablespoons salt

1 large bell pepper, chopped

Tabasco® to taste

3 bay leaves

1 teaspoon thyme

½ teaspoon basil

1 pound fresh lump crab meat

8 boiled crabs, cleaned and halved (optional)

3 pounds small or medium raw shrimp, peeled

Optional: Tabasco® and cayenne to taste

$=$ CHEF NOTES $=$

_____

_____

_____

_____

_____

_____

_____

_____

_____

_____

_____

_____

_____

_____

_____

_____

_____

_____

_____

_____

_____

1954
FLAUTAS

SERVES 12

Directions

1. In a double boiler, combine refried beans, cumin, garlic salt and Monterey Jack cheese. Stir and heat over hot water until cheese melts. Crumble beef and sausage in a skillet and cook but do not brown. Drain grease.

2. Add 2 cans green chile salsa and cook until most of the liquid has evaporated. Spread each tortilla with hot bean mixture. Spread meat over beans. Roll tortillas and place seam side down in a single layer in a large well-greased baking pan. Pour remaining cans of green chile salsa on top. Sprinkle with Colby cheese, tomatoes and green onion tops.

3. Bake uncovered for 20 minutes at 350 degrees. Serve each flauta on a bed of shredded lettuce and top with a dollop of sour cream.

SOURCE: COLORADO CACHE WITH
ADAPTATIONS BY
MRS. GERALDINE WILLIAMS BROOKS

2 (16-ounce) cans of refried beans

¼ teaspoon garlic salt

2 pounds ground beef

4 (7-ounce) cans green chile salsa

4 cups grated Colby Longhorn cheese

6 cups shredded lettuce

1½ cup grated Monterey Jack cheese

3 large tomatoes, peeled and chopped

¾ teaspoon ground cumin

1 pound ground chorizo

2 cups sour cream

12 white flour tortillas

½ cup sliced green onion tops

2 cups sour cream

=CHEF NOTES=

_____

_____

_____

_____

_____

_____

_____

_____

_____

_____

_____

_____

_____

_____

_____

_____

_____

_____

_____

_____

_____

_____

_____

_____

_____

CHICKEN TETRAZZINI

SERVES 12

Directions

1. Boil hen with an onion and 2 or 3 stalks celery. Meanwhile, sauté the green peppers and onions in the 3 tablespoons of butter. When chicken is tender, allow it to cool, then strip meat from bones, reserving broth. Skim fat from broth, add salt and then cook spaghetti in broth.

2. While hen is boiling make cream sauce with first four ingredients, then add remaining seven ingredients. Mix together chicken, cooked spaghetti, cream cheese sauce, bell peppers and onions, mushrooms and pimentos.

3. Pour mixture into casserole pan. Heat at 350 degrees until heated through. May be frozen ahead, thawed, then heated.

SOURCE: MRS. H. EDWIN MCGLASSON

1 hen (5 or 6 pounds)

3 large green peppers, chopped

3 large onions, chopped

3 tablespoons butter

1 cup finely chopped broccoli (optional)

1 large package spaghetti

1 or 2 cans mushrooms

1 jar chopped pimentos

3 stalks celery

Cream Cheese Sauce:

8 tablespoons butter

8 tablespoons flour

4 cups milk

1 teaspoon salt

½ pound cheddar cheese, grated

½ pound American cheese, grated

1 tablespoon lemon juice

3 teaspoons dry mustard

1 teaspoon salt

¼ cup cooking sherry

Red pepper to taste

= CHEF NOTES =

_____

_____

_____

_____

_____

_____

_____

_____

_____

_____

_____

_____

_____

_____

_____

_____

_____

_____

_____

_____

CRAWFISH STEW

SERVES 6

Directions

1. Heat butter in saucepan. Add flour and make medium brown roux. Add onions, bell pepper, garlic, celery and tomato sauce. Simmer 5 minutes.

2. Add crawfish fat, water, seasonings (including Tabasco® and Worcestershire sauce), lemon slice and crawfish. Simmer for 30 minutes. Serve over rice if desired.

SOURCE: MRS. GERALDINE WILLIAMS BROOKS

1 stick butter

3 tablespoons crawfish fat

1 cup chopped celery

½ cup chopped bell pepper

2 onions, chopped

1¼ cups water

1 dash Tabasco® sauce

½ cup tomato sauce sauce

2 pounds crawfish tails

2 tablespoons flour

1 thin lemon slice

¼ teaspoon white pepper

½ teaspoon red pepper

2 teaspoons minced garlic

1 tablespoon Worcestershire

= CHEF NOTES =

_____

_____

_____

_____

_____

_____

_____

_____

_____

_____

_____

_____

_____

_____

_____

_____

_____

_____

_____

_____

Directions

1. Combine pepper, garlic powder, Creole seasoning and Worcestershire sauce, rub on all sides of ribs. Soak wood chunks in water for 30 minutes. Prepare charcoal fire in grill, drain wood chunks and place on coals. Cook ribs covered with grill lid over medium coals (300 to 350 degrees) about 3 hours, turning ribs after 1 hour.

2. Baste with Grill Basting Sauce after 2 hours. Turn ribs once more after basting. Serve ribs with The Sauce.

Grill Basting Sauce

Combine all ingredients in a saucepan; cook over medium heat 1 hour. Yields 6 cups.

Ribs

8 pounds pork spareribs

1 tablespoon garlic powder

1 tablespoon Worcestershire sauce

Grill basting sauce

2 tablespoons pepper

1 tablespoon Creole seasoning

Hickory wood chunks

The Sauce

Grill Basting Sauce

¼ cup firmly packed brown sugar

¼ cup prepared mustard

2 tablespoons ground black pepper

2 ¾ cups red wine vinegar

2 to 4 tablespoons salt

¼ cup Worcestershire sauce

¼ cup ketchup

2 tablespoons dried crushed red pepper

1 ¾ cup dry white wine

continued on next page

The Sauce

1 tablespoon butter or margarine

½ tablespoon minced garlic

½ cup white vinegar

¼ cup steak seasoning

1 tablespoon Cajun seasoning

1 medium onion, finely chopped

1 cup ketchup

¼ cup fresh lemon juice

2 tablespoons brown sugar

2 tablespoons liquid smoke

The Sauce

1. Melt butter in large skillet over medium-high heat, add onion, and cook, stirring constantly until tender.

2. Add garlic and remaining ingredients, reduce heat, and simmer about 15 minutes. Yield 2 ½ cups.

SOURCE: SOUTHERN LIVING; JUSTICE AND MRS. OSCAR ADAMS OF BIRMINGHAM, AL

= CHEF NOTES =

_____

_____

_____

SOUTHERN BUTTERMILK BISCUITS

SERVES 10 TO 12

¼ cup shortening

1 cup buttermilk

⅓ stick melted butter (optional)

2 cups self-rising flour

½ teaspoon salt

1 teaspoon sugar

Directions

1. In large bowl combine flour, salt, and sugar. Cut shortening into flour mixture with a pastry blender or large fork until crumbly. Add buttermilk to mixture and stir until moistened.

2. Turn dough on a lightly floured surface and knead gently. Roll out dough on floured surface to 1½ inch thickness. Cut out dough using 2½ inch round cookie cutter dipped in flour (do not twist cutter) and place on lightly greased cookie sheet.

3. Bake at 425 degrees for about 14 minutes or until golden brown. Remove from oven and brush hot biscuits with melted butter if desired.

SOURCE: MRS. GERALDINE WILLIAMS BROOKS

= CHEF NOTES =

SKILLET CORNBREAD

SERVES 8

2 cups self-rising cornmeal

1 egg

2 cups buttermilk

⅓ cup butter

1 tablespoon sugar

1 pinch of salt

Directions

1. Pre-heat oven to 425 degrees. In a large bowl combine self-rising cornmeal, buttermilk, sugar, salt, and egg and mix thoroughly (mixture will remain slightly lumpy).

2. Add butter to large cast iron skillet (approximately 10") and melt butter in oven. Evenly coat butter in skillet. Add cornbread mixture to skillet and bake at 425 degrees for 20 minutes or until golden brown. Remove cornbread from skillet and cool.

SOURCE: MRS. GERALDINE WILLIAMS BROOKS

= CHEF NOTES =

1960
SIMPLE & DELICIOUS HOLIDAY YAMS

SERVES 6 TO 8

8 small Louisiana yams, peeled

2 quarts water

1 cup sugar

¼ pound butter

2 tablespoons pure vanilla extract

3 whole cloves

Directions

1. Place yams in a 12-inch diameter saucepan. Add water to cover yams by ¼ inch. Bring to a rolling boil then reduce to high simmer and cook 30–35 minutes or until yams are fork tender but not overcooked. Drain all but ¼ inch water.

2. Add sugar, butter, vanilla and cloves. Continue to simmer until a simple syrup is achieved and yams have absorbed most of the liquid (about 30 minutes). Baste yams from time to time with the simple syrup. Serve 1 yam per guest with syrup.

**Note: Most holiday yam recipes contain numerous spices and marshmallow topping. This recipe may seem much more boring, but even with fewer ingredients, these yams are magnificent. Yams should all be about the same size so they cook uniformly. Smaller yams are best for this recipe since 1 yam will serve as 1 portion.

SOURCE: CHEF JOHN FOLSE

= CHEF NOTES =

CREAMY MACARONI & CHEESE

MAKES 2 CASSEROLES: EACH SERVES 4

1 cup Panko breadcrumbs

6 tablespoons all-purpose flour

1 garlic clove, minced

4 cups whole milk

1 pound Colby cheese, shredded
(4 cups)

1 ounce parmesan cheese, grated
(½ cup)

2 tablespoons unsalted butter,
melted, plus 6 tablespoons
unsalted butter seasoned with
salt & pepper

1 pound elbow macaroni

2 teaspoons dry mustard

¼ teaspoon cayenne pepper

2¼ cups chicken broth

8 ounces extra sharp cheddar
cheese, shredded (2 cups)

Directions

1. Adjust oven rack to middle position and
   heat to 350 degrees. Toss panko with melted
   butter and season with salt and pepper.
   Spread evenly on rimmed baking sheet and
   bake until golden brown, about 10 minutes;
   set aside.

2. Bring 4 quarts of water to boil in large pot.
   Add macaroni and 1 tablespoon salt and
   cook, stirring often until nearly dente. Drain
   macaroni, rinse with cold water, and drain
   again leaving macaroni slightly wet; leave in
   colander.

3. Dry now-empty pot and add remaining 6 tablespoons of butter and melt over
   medium heat. Stir in flour, mustard, garlic,
   and cayenne and cook for 1 minute. Slowly
   whisk in milk and broth until smooth. Bring
   to simmer and cook, whisking often until
   thickened, about 15 minutes.

4. Off heat, gradually whisk in Colby, cheddar, parmesan, 1 teaspoon salt, and pinch of pepper. Let cool completely, about 30 minutes. Stir macaroni into sauce breaking up any clumps. Divide macaroni mixture evenly between 2 greased 8-inch square disposable aluminum pans. Sprinkle evenly with toasted panko. To serve 1 casserole right away, bake uncovered on aluminum foil-lined rimmed baking sheet in 375-degree oven until sauce is bubbling around edges, 20 to 25 minutes. Let cool for 10 minutes before serving.

To Store:

Wrap pans tightly with plastic wrap and cover with foil. Freeze up to 1 month. (Do not thaw before reheating.)

SOURCE: THE MAKE-AHEAD COOK BY AMERICA'S TEST KITCHEN

= CHEF NOTES =

_____

_____

_____

_____

_____

_____

_____

_____

_____

_____

_____

_____

_____

_____

_____

_____

_____

_____

_____

_____

_____

_____

CHICKEN POT PIE

SERVES 4

Directions

1. In a heavy saucepan, sauté carrot, celery, onion and peas in vegetable oil until onion is translucent. Add chicken and cook 2 minutes. Add chicken stock and simmer 15 minutes. Add potatoes and cook until potatoes are tender. Add heavy cream and cook until mixture thickens slightly. Stir in sherry, salt, and pepper.

2. Preheat oven to 375 degrees. In a glass pie pan fit one pie crust along the bottom of the pan. Spoon chicken mixture into pie crust. Cover with second pie crust and cut off excess along the outside of the pie pan.

3. Press edges of upper and lower pie crust together and crimp with fork. Brush top of pie crust with egg wash and prick with fork. Bake until golden brown about 25 to 30 minutes.

4. Garnish with parsley when serving.

SOURCE: THE DELTA QUEEN COOKBOOK/
CYNTHIA LEJEUNE NOBLES
WITH ADAPTATIONS BY
MRS. GERALDINE WILLIAMS BROOKS

1 carrot, diced (½-inch pieces)

½ cup diced yellow onions (½-inch pieces)

2 tablespoons vegetable oil

2 ½ cups chicken stock

½ cup diced potatoes

1 tablespoon sherry

1 rib celery, diced ½-inch pieces

¼ cup frozen green peas

2 large boneless, skinless chicken breasts cut into bite sized pieces

½ cup heavy cream

Salt and pepper

Egg wash (1 egg beaten with 1 tablespoon of water)

2 rolled Pillsbury® Pie Crusts

Chopped fresh parsley for garnish

= CHEF NOTES =

_____

_____

_____

_____

_____

_____

_____

_____

_____

_____

_____

_____

_____

_____

_____

_____

_____

_____

_____

_____

_____

CAJUN BLAST PORK ROAST

SERVES 4 TO 6

Directions

1. For vegetable blend, chop 2 medium onions, 1 bell pepper and 10–12 whole garlic pods. Season all vegetables well with Cajun Blast Seasoning and soak in Cajun Blast Garlic Butter Basting Spray and 2 tablespoons of Worcestershire sauce.

2. Make slits on all sides of the roast. Make the cavity large enough to put your index finger in (about ½-inch diameter and 3 to 4 inches deep). Stuff holes with the vegetable blend. Season roast well with Cajun Blast Creole Seasoning. Coat pot with Cajun Blast Garlic Butter Basting Spray and brown roast well on all sides in Dutch oven.

3. Finely chop remaining 2 onions and 1 bell pepper. After browning roast, add finely chopped onions, bell peppers, and Ro-tel® tomatoes and fill Dutch oven with water to three-quarters up the side of the roast.

4 medium onions

1 whole bulb garlic

Cajun Blast Creole Seasoning

1 bunch parsley, chopped

1 (14-ounce) can Ro-tel® tomatoes

Cajun Blast Garlic Butter Basting Spray

2 bell peppers

1 Boston butt pork roast

1 (16-ounce) jar of roux

1 bunch green onions, chopped

2 tablespoons Worcestershire sauce

continued on next page

4. Simmer for 2 ½ hours with the lid on. Check every 30 minutes, basting with Cajun Blast Garlic Butter Basting Spray.

5. After 2 ½ hours, add green onions, parsley and roux. Cook an additional 10 to 15 minutes until roux thickens. Serve over rice.

SOURCE: QUALITY SALES, INC., CROWLEY, LA

= CHEF NOTES =

_____

_____

_____

_____

_____

_____

_____

_____

_____

_____

_____

_____

_____

_____

_____

_____

_____

_____

_____

_____

_____

_____

_____

══ 1964 ══
BAKED BEANS

SERVES 10

3 bacon slices

3 (15-ounce) cans pork and beans

3 tablespoons brown sugar

1 small onion, finely chopped

½ cup barbecue sauce

2 tablespoons prepared mustard

Directions

1. Cook bacon in a skillet until crisp; remove bacon and drain on paper towels reserving 2 tablespoons of drippings in skillet. Crumble bacon and set aside.

2. Sauté onion in hot drippings in skillet until tender. Stir together onion, beans, and next 3 ingredients in a lightly greased 2-quart baking dish. Sprinkle with bacon.

3. Bake at 350 degrees for 1 hour.

SOURCE: SOUTHERN LIVING FAVORITES

= CHEF NOTES =

1965
CAJUN BBQ COCKTAIL MEATBALLS

SERVES 10

2 pounds ground meat

2 tablespoons Worcestershire sauce

2 tablespoons dried parsley

½ cup diced onion

½ cup milk

3 teaspoons hot sauce

4 tablespoons Cajun seasoning

2 teaspoons garlic powder

½ cup breadcrumbs

2 eggs

For the Sauce:

2 cups BBQ sauce of your choice

2 tablespoons brown sugar

2 cups peach or apricot jam

Dash of cayenne

Directions

1. Preheat oven to 350 degrees and spray a cookie sheet (or 2) with non-stick spray. Mix all meatball ingredients together and form into golf ball sized balls. Place on greased cookie sheet about ½-inch apart.

2. Bake for 30–40 minutes until cooked through. Mix the sauce ingredients. Mix ingredients together and heat in a medium saucepan. Once hot, toss with cooked meatballs and serve.

TIP: Make the meatballs and the sauce the day before and refrigerate. On the day that you plan on serving the meatballs, throw the meatballs into a Crockpot, and then pour the sauce over them. Heat on low for a few hours until ready to serve!

SOURCE: ALL RECIPES

= CHEF NOTES =

_____

_____

_____

_____

_____

_____

_____

_____

_____

_____

_____

_____

_____

_____

_____

_____

_____

_____

_____

_____

WAFFLE OMELET

SERVES 1

2 large eggs

½ teaspoon Creole seasoning

¼ teaspoon black pepper

2 tablespoons milk

4 slices bacon

¼ cup shredded mild cheddar cheese

3 tablespoons chives

Directions

1. Cook 4 slices of bacon beforehand and crumble into bits.

2. Preheat waffle iron and spray with non-stick cooking spray.

3. Whisk together eggs, milk, creole seasoning and pepper in a bowl; stir in cheese.

4. Pour in waffle iron and cook for about 5 minutes or until your desired texture.

5. Top with chives and serve.

SOURCE: UNKNOWN

= CHEF NOTES =

_____
_____
_____
_____
_____
_____
_____
_____
_____
_____
_____
_____
_____
_____
_____
_____
_____
_____
_____
_____

THE BEST PUNCH

MAKES 5 GALLON BUCKET

4 large cans pineapple juice

3 (2-liter) bottles of ginger ale or Sprite (your choice)

3 canisters of Kool-Aid® Fruit Punch

Directions

Mix all ingredients in 5-gallon drink cooler. Fill with water and ice. Serve.

SOURCE: MRS. GERALDINE WILLIAMS BROOKS

= CHEF NOTES =

EXCELLENT STUFFED PEPPERS

6 SERVINGS

6 bell peppers

4 garlic cloves, minced

6 green onion tops and bottoms, thinly sliced

½ stick butter for sautéing

3 tablespoons tomato paste

1 teaspoon garlic salt

¼ teaspoon black pepper

1 teaspoon dried oregano

¼ teaspoon anise seed

10 fresh mushrooms, slightly chopped

⅓ cup grated parmesan cheese

½ cup grated cheddar cheese

6 pats butter for topping

1 cup rice, cooked

2 white onions, finely chopped

2 ribs celery, finely chopped

1½ lbs. ground chuck

1 beef bouillon cube, crushed

¼ teaspoon cayenne pepper

½ teaspoon dried sweet basil

½ teaspoon salt

¼ teaspoon fennel seed

6 sprigs fresh parsley, chopped or 1 tablespoon dried parsley

Directions

1. Pre-heat oven to 350 degrees. Clean and devein peppers. Boil peppers until color changes from bright green to olive green and they are about half done. Note: you don't want them limp when you take them out of the water because they will tear up while you are stuffing them. Remove and drain upside down on paper towels.

2. Cook rice and set aside.

3. Mince garlic, chop and slice onions, and chop celery. Sauté in butter in deep sided skillet. Add ground meat and tomato paste. Continue simmering. Crush bouillon cube and add with garlic salt, cayenne pepper, black pepper, sweet basil, oregano, salt, and fennel. Mix well.

4. Add and mix in mushrooms and parsley. Slowly and evenly add cheeses and mix well, simmering all the while. After a few minutes, removed from heat and toss with cooked rice. Note: you can use the same skillet.

5. Stuff peppers gently but do not pack. Top each pepper with a pat of butter and place side by side in Pyrex or suitable cooking utensil. Add about ½ inch of water to the bottom of the dish. Tightly cover with foil and cook in pre-heated 350-degree oven for 20 to 30 minutes. Remove cover and continue to cook until tops are slightly browned.

SOURCE: MRS. GERALDINE WILLIAMS BROOKS;
INSPIRED BY UNKNOWN SOURCE

= CHEF NOTES =

_____
_____
_____
_____
_____
_____
_____
_____
_____
_____
_____
_____
_____
_____
_____
_____
_____
_____
_____
_____
_____

DEVILED EGGS

SERVES 12

Directions

Peel and halve eggs then set aside. Place cooked egg yolks in medium-sized bowl and mix with remaining ingredients (except for the paprika). Make sure mixture is creamy. Fill egg white halves with mixture.

Note: pastry filling bags work well for this step. Use paprika to dust tops of filled halves. Refrigerate until you are ready to serve.

SOURCE: MRS. GERALDINE WILLIAMS BROOKS

1 dozen hard boiled eggs

⅛ cup dill pickle relish

⅛ cup mustard

3 dashes of salt

3 dashes of black pepper

3 dashes of paprika

1 tablespoon. chopped green onions

⅛ cup mustard

1 tablespoon sugar

2 dashes of creole seasoning

3 dashes of red pepper

= CHEF NOTES =

SPAGHETTI WITH CRAWFISH AND RED SAUCE

SERVES 4 TO 6

Directions

1. Heat olive oil in heavy pot and add the onion, bell pepper and garlic. Cook over medium heat stirring occasionally until softened; about 10 minutes. Add the tomato puree, chicken stock, wine and cane syrup. Season with salt, pepper, Creole seasoning, and hot sauce. Simmer, stirring occasionally for about 30 minutes.

2. Add crawfish and chopped parsley. Simmer for an additional 20 minutes. Adjust seasonings if needed.

3. Cook the spaghetti according to the package instructions. Drain and transfer to serving bowl. Add the sauce and toss. Serve with grated parmesan cheese.

SOURCE: LOUISIANA LIFE

2 tablespoons olive oil

1 bell pepper, chopped

1 (28-ounce) can tomato puree

½ cup white wine

Coarse salt and freshly ground black pepper to taste

2 tablespoon chopped parsley

Freshly grated parmesan

1 pound cooked and peeled crawfish tails with fat

1 medium onion

4 cloves garlic, minced

½ cup chicken stock or broth

1 tablespoon cane syrup

1 pound spaghetti

Optional: Creole seasoning and hot sauce to taste.

= CHEF NOTES =

RED BEANS AND RICE

SERVES 8 TO 10

Directions

1. Place red beans in colander and rinse; pick out any bad ones. In a large pot sauté onions, garlic, bell pepper, celery and green onions in a drizzle of olive oil to release flavor. In a medium to large pot add 9 cups of water and stir in all remaining ingredients except the sausage. Bring it to a boil.

2. Lower heat to a simmer and simmer for about 3 hours. Add sausage and simmer an additional 3 minutes or until water becomes thick and smooth. Beans should also be tender at this time. Serve over rice.

SOURCE: MRS. GERALDINE WILLIAMS BROOKS

1 pound dried red beans

9 cups of water

2 bay leaves

1 pound smoked sausage

2 cups chopped onions

1 tablespoon salt

4 cloves of minced garlic

2 smoked pork neck bones or ½ pound smoked Tasso

1 bell pepper, chopped

2 celery stalks, chopped

1 drizzle of olive oil

⅛ teaspoon thyme

2 teaspoons black pepper

1 teaspoon red pepper

1 bunch finely chopped green onions

Creole seasoning to taste

= CHEF NOTES =

_____

_____

_____

_____

_____

_____

_____

_____

_____

_____

_____

_____

_____

_____

_____

_____

_____

_____

_____

_____

_____

_____

JUICY SEASONED BURGERS

SERVES 6

Directions

1. Combine all ingredients in a large bowl. Mix well. Make 6 patties. Lightly spray cast iron skillet with cooking spray (just enough to prevent sticking).

2. Cook burgers in skillet on medium to low heat until desired internal temperature. For medium well burgers this should take approximately 5 minutes per side.

SOURCE: MRS. GERALDINE WILLIAMS BROOKS

1 pound lean ground beef

½ cup Progresso Garlic & Herb breadcrumbs

¼ teaspoon salt

1 tablespoon Creole seasoning

¼ teaspoon onion powder

1 egg beaten

1 teaspoon Worcestershire sauce

¼ teaspoon pepper

¼ teaspoon garlic powder

=CHEF NOTES=

SOUTHERN CORNBREAD DRESSING

SERVES 16 TO 18; CHILL 8 HRS. PRIOR TO BAKING

Directions

1. Place ½ cup butter in a 13 x 9-inch pan; heat in oven at 425 degrees for 4 minutes.

2. Combine cornmeal and next 5 ingredients; whisk in 3 eggs and buttermilk.

3. Pour hot butter into batter, stirring until blended. Pour batter into pan.

4. Bake at 425 degrees for 30 minutes or until golden brown. Cool.

5. Crumble cornbread into a large bowl; stir in breadcrumbs and set aside.

6. Melt remaining ½ cup butter in a large skillet over medium heat; add onions and celery, and sauté until tender. Stir in sage, and sauté 1 more minute.

1 cup butter or margarine, divided

1 cup all-purpose flour

2 teaspoons baking powder

1 teaspoon baking soda

3 cups buttermilk

2 medium onions, diced (2 cups)

½ cup finely chopped fresh sage

1 tablespoon pepper

3 cups white cornmeal

2 tablespoons sugar

1½ teaspoons salt

7 large eggs, divided

3 cups soft breadcrumbs

1 bunch celery, diced (3 cups)

6 (10 ½-ounce) cans condensed chicken broth, undiluted

continued on next page

7. Stir vegetables, remaining 4 eggs, chicken broth, and pepper into cornbread mixture; pour evenly into 1 lightly greased 13 x 9-inch baking dish and 1 lightly greased 8-inch square baking dish. Cover and chill 8 hours.

8. Bake, uncovered, at 375 degrees for 35 to 40 minutes or until golden brown.

SOURCE: VALERIE FRASER; TASTE OF THE SOUTH

= CHEF NOTES =

_____

_____

_____

_____

_____

_____

_____

_____

_____

_____

_____

_____

_____

_____

_____

_____

_____

_____

_____

_____

_____

_____

_____

RICE DRESSING

SERVES 12 TO 14

1 tablespoon oil

2 ½ pounds lean ground beef

1 bell pepper, chopped

1 (14 ½-ounce) can chicken broth

Salt, black pepper and cayenne pepper to taste

¼ green onions, chopped

1 tablespoon Creole seasoning

½ teaspoon onion powder

1 tablespoon flour

2 medium onions, chopped

3 ribs celery, chopped

1 teaspoon Kitchen Bouquet

3 cups raw rice, cooked

¼ cup parsley, chopped

½ teaspoon garlic powder

Directions

1. In heavy skillet make a roux of flour and oil. Cook until golden brown and set aside.

2. In a Dutch oven, cook meat until no longer pink. Pour off pan drippings. Add onions, bell pepper and celery. Sauté until soft. Add roux, chicken broth and Kitchen Bouquet. The Kitchen Bouquet will give it a nice brown color.

3. Season with salt, creole seasoning, garlic powder, onion powder, black pepper and cayenne pepper to taste. Simmer over low heat, uncovered for 25 minutes.

4. Check seasoning in meat mixture. You want this to be well seasoned. Begin adding the cooked rice, parsley and green onions. You want the dressing to be moist, so add the rice by large spoonfuls. You may not need the full pot of rice. Stir to blend well. Keep pot covered so that rice will stay moist.

SOURCE: MRS. GERALDINE WILLIAMS BROOKS

= CHEF NOTES =

_____

_____

_____

_____

_____

_____

_____

_____

_____

_____

_____

_____

_____

_____

_____

_____

_____

_____

_____

_____

_____

_____

_____

BEEF STROGANOFF

SERVES 4

1 pound steak strips

1 medium onion, chopped

1 cup sour cream

1 small can of mushrooms, drained

1 tablespoon melted margarine

Cooking oil

1 clove garlic, crushed

1 (10 ¾-ounce) can cream of mushroom soup

2 tablespoons ketchup

3 cups cooked egg noodles

2 tablespoons Worcestershire sauce

Directions

In a 10- or 12-inch skillet, brown meat strips in a small amount of hot oil. Add onion and garlic; cook until just tender. Combine sour cream, Worcestershire sauce, soup, ketchup and drained mushrooms. Pour over meat and heat through. Toss noodles with margarine. Serve sauce over noodles.

SOURCE: JOANIE LEBLANC, DENHAM SPRINGS, LA

= CHEF NOTES =

OYSTERS AND ANGEL HAIR PASTA

SERVES 6 TO 8

1 quart fresh oysters

12 cloves garlic, minced

2 bunches green onions, chopped (only tops)

Black pepper, to taste

1 (12-ounce) package angel hair pasta

4 tablespoons olive oil

½ cup chopped fresh parsley

Salt, to taste

Cayenne pepper, to taste

Directions

Drain oysters and cook in oil just until they begin to curl. Add garlic, parsley and green onions and cook until vegetables are tender. Season to taste with salt, black pepper and cayenne pepper. Serve immediately over cooked angel hair pasta.

SOURCE: SALLY SYLVESTER

= CHEF NOTES =

BAKED GRITS AND GREENS WITH BACON

SERVES 8 TO 10

1 teaspoon garlic salt

⅓ cup finely chopped red onion

2 large eggs

1 ½ cups (6 ounces) shredded parmesan cheese

½ teaspoon freshly ground pepper

1 (10-ounce) package frozen spinach, chopped, thawed, drained

1 cup uncooked quick-cooking grits

5 tablespoons butter divided

½ cup bottled creamy Caesar dressing

¼ cup coarsely crushed garlic flavored croutons

1 (3-ounce) package real bacon bits

Directions

1. Preheat oven to 350 degrees. Bring garlic salt and 4 cups water to a boil in a large saucepan over medium-high heat; gradually stir in grits. Reduce heat to medium, and cook, stirring often, 5 minutes or until thickened. Remove from heat and stir in onion and 3 tablespoons of butter.

2. Whisk together eggs, bacon bits, spinach, parmesan cheese, and ground pepper in a large bowl. Stir about one-fourth of grits mixture gradually into egg mixture; add remaining grits mixture, stirring constantly. Pour into a lightly greased 13 x 9-inch baking dish.

3. Melt remaining 2 tablespoons of butter and toss with coarsely crushed croutons; sprinkle over grits mixture.

4. Bake at 350 degrees for 30 to 35 minutes or until mixture is set and croutons are golden brown.

SOURCE: SOUTHERN LIVING

= CHEF NOTES =

_____

_____

_____

_____

_____

_____

_____

_____

_____

_____

_____

_____

_____

_____

_____

_____

_____

_____

_____

_____

_____

1978
CRACKLING CORNBREAD

SERVES 12

1 ½ cups corn meal

¼ cup flour

1 teaspoon soda

2 cups buttermilk

1 egg

1 cup finely cut cracklings or
   1 teaspoon salt crumbled crisp
   bacon

Directions

1. Sift together dry ingredients. Add butter-milk and egg, stirring until well mixed. Season cracklings with additional salt to taste and fold them in last. Pour batter into very hot, well-greased iron skillet or muffin pan (12 muffins).

2. Bake in 450 degree oven for about 23 minutes.

SOURCE: MRS. ANTHONY P. ACOSTA
ROSENEATH; JACKSON, LA

= CHEF NOTES =

_____

_____

_____

_____

_____

_____

_____

_____

_____

_____

_____

_____

_____

_____

_____

_____

_____

_____

_____

_____

_____

_____

"PANAMA LIMITED" FRENCH TOAST

SERVES 2

2 eggs

3 cups shortening

½ cup milk

Confectioners' sugar

2 slices bread, cut 1½ inch thick, crust trimmed then cut diagonally

Directions

1. Beat eggs well then mix in the milk and beat again. Dip bread slices in egg and milk mixture.

Note: It is not necessary to soak bread, but this can be done according to preference.

2. Fry in hot shortening (about 3 cups of shortening in a medium sized fry pan). Brown on both sides. Drain the cooked toast. Sprinkle liberally with confectioners' sugar and serve hot.

SOURCE: ILLINOIS CENTRAL RAILROAD

= CHEF NOTES =

BAKED CUSHAW

SERVES 4

1 medium cushaw

2 cups sugar

1 teaspoon vanilla

½ teaspoon baking powder

2 eggs

2 tablespoons flour

½ pound butter

Nutmeg to taste

Directions

Cut cushaw into pieces, scrape out seed, and boil until tender. Remove peeling. Mix cushaw with the rest of the ingredients. Place in baking dish and bake in 350-degree oven until brown on top.

Note: Cushaw is a type of squash.

SOURCE: MRS. EDWARD WALL

= CHEF NOTES =

_____

_____

_____

_____

_____

_____

_____

_____

_____

_____

_____

_____

_____

_____

_____

_____

_____

_____

_____

_____

CHICKEN SPAGHETTI

SERVES 6

1 large hen

3 cloves garlic, chopped

1 bell pepper, chopped

½ bunch parsley, chopped

1 can tomato sauce

½ can tomato paste

1 bay leaf

2 tablespoons Worcestershire
sauce

1 pack spaghetti

2 large onions, chopped

4 ribs celery, chopped

1 bunch green onions, chopped

2 tablespoons bacon drippings

1 can tomato soup

Salt and pepper to taste

Dash of hot sauce

2 cups chicken broth

Directions

1. Boil hen in seasoned water (enough water to cover). Save broth. Remove bones from chicken and cut into large pieces. In a large heavy pot sauté onions, garlic, celery, bell pepper, and green onions in hot bacon drippings, adding the parsley as they cook. Add tomato sauce, soup, paste, and seasonings. Thin the mixture with the broth and add the boned chicken.

2. Cover and simmer for about 1 hour or until the sauce has thickened. Follow cooking instructions on spaghetti package and serve over spaghetti.

SOURCE: MRS. E. O. SPILLER

= CHEF NOTES =

_____

_____

_____

_____

_____

_____

_____

_____

_____

_____

_____

_____

_____

_____

_____

_____

_____

_____

_____

_____

_____

_____

MIGHTY GOOD MEAT LOAF

SERVES 8 TO 10

1½ cups spaghetti sauce, divided

½ cup Italian-seasoned breadcrumbs

1 large egg

¼ teaspoon pepper

1½ tablespoons white vinegar

2 teaspoons Worcestershire sauce

½ teaspoon onion powder

1½ pounds lean ground beef

1 small onion, minced

1½ teaspoons salt

1 tablespoon brown sugar

1 tablespoon prepared mustard

½ teaspoon garlic powder

1 pinch of oregano

Directions

1. Stir together ½ cup spaghetti sauce, ground beef, breadcrumbs, onion, egg, salt, pepper, onion powder, garlic powder and oregano just until combined. Shape mixture into 2 (8-inch) loaves, and place in lightly greased 13 x 9-inch baking dish.

2. Bake at 350 degrees for 25 minutes.

3. Stir together remaining spaghetti sauce, brown sugar, and remaining ingredients. Pour sauce over meat loaves and bake an additional 25 minutes until center of beef is no longer pink.

4. Let stand 10 minutes prior to serving.

SOURCE: MRS. GERALDINE WILLIAMS BROOKS; INSPIRED BY MARGARET MCNEIL OF MEMPHIS, TN

= CHEF NOTES =

_____

_____

_____

_____

_____

_____

_____

_____

_____

_____

_____

_____

_____

_____

_____

_____

_____

_____

_____

_____

_____

_____

SHRIMP STUFFED EGGPLANT

SERVES 2

1 medium eggplant

8 ounce can mushrooms

2 tablespoons butter

½ pound raw shrimp, peeled, deveined (cut in 1-inch pieces)

2 tablespoons all-purpose flour

2 cans pimentos, chopped

Boiling, saltwater

2 green onions

½ cup evaporated milk

1 teaspoon garlic powder

1 teaspoon salt

Black pepper to taste

Topping:

2 tablespoons Italian breadcrumbs, mixed with 1 teaspoon melted butter

1 tablespoon grated parmesan cheese

2 slices crispy fried bacon crumbled

Directions

1. Cut large lengthwise slice of eggplant. Remove pulp and cut into cubes. Cook 10 minutes in small amount of boiling salted water. Reserve shell. While eggplant is cooking, brown mushrooms, onion and bell pepper in butter.

2. Add shrimp and cook over low heat until shrimp turns pink. Stir in garlic powder, flour, salt and pepper. Add well-drained eggplant, milk and pimento. Fill shell. Top with last 3 ingredients.

3. Bake 30 minutes at 350 degrees.

SOURCE: UNKNOWN

= CHEF NOTES =

_____

_____

_____

_____

_____

_____

_____

_____

_____

_____

_____

_____

_____

_____

_____

_____

_____

_____

_____

_____

_____

_____

PORK CHOP CASSEROLE

SERVES 4

4 pork chops

¾ cup rice

1 tomato, sliced

1 bell pepper, sliced

1 onion, sliced

1 can beef bouillon

Directions

1. Place raw rice in bottom of casserole. Brown pork chops in skillet then arrange on top of rice. Place slice of onion, tomato, and pepper on top of each pork chop. Pour can of beef bouillon on top.

2. Cover casserole and bake in oven at 375 degrees for about an hour. Add water if needed.

SOURCE: MRS. R. W. SCHEFFY

= CHEF NOTES =

_____

_____

_____

_____

_____

_____

_____

_____

_____

_____

_____

_____

_____

_____

_____

_____

_____

_____

_____

_____

_____

_____

CHICKEN AND DUMPLINGS

SERVES 6 TO 8

For the broth:

2 chickens (4 pounds each),
   backs removed and cut into
   8 pieces each

1 large onion, coarsely chopped

6 cups water

2 bay leaves

1½ teaspoons salt

For the dumplings:

2 cups all-purpose flour

4 teaspoons baking powder

1 teaspoon salt

3 tablespoons butter

1 cup milk

7 tablespoons butter

10 tablespoons all-purpose flour

½ cup frozen green peas, thawed

Salt and freshly ground black
   pepper

¼ cup dry white wine

2 teaspoons Essence, recipe
   follows

1 teaspoon fresh thyme leaves

Directions

Cut chicken backs, necks and wings into 1-inch pieces.

Prepare the broth:

In a large pot, combine the chicken, onions, water, bay leaves and salt. Bring to a boil. Reduce heat to low and simmer, partially covered, until the chicken is tender, about 45 minutes. Remove the chicken pieces and set aside. Discard the chicken backs, necks, and wings. When the chicken pieces have cooled, remove the meat from the bones in chunks and set aside. Discard the skin and bones. Strain the broth and discard the vegetables.

Prepare the dumplings:

1. In a medium bowl, mix the flour, baking powder, and salt together. In a small saucepan over low heat, bring the butter and milk to a simmer. Stir the butter and milk mixture into the dry ingredients with a fork and stir until the mixture just comes together. On a

lightly floured surface, roll the dough out to a ⅛-inch thickness. Cut into long strips 1-inch wide. Transfer to a large plate or baking sheet and cover with plastic wrap. Refrigerate until ready to use.

2. In the cleaned Dutch oven, melt the butter over medium heat. Whisk in the flour and cook until golden-brown, 3 to 4 minutes. While whisking, add the wine, the reserved chicken broth, Essence, and thyme.

3. Cook until thickened, about 5 minutes, then add the celery, carrots, and onion. Cook until the vegetables are tender-crisp, about 15 minutes. Add the reserved chicken meat, heavy cream, and peas. Season with salt (if necessary), and add black pepper, to taste.

4. Place the dumplings on top of the chicken mixture and gently stir into the hot liquid. Cover and simmer until the dumplings are cooked through, about 10 minutes. Gently stir in the parsley. Serve in large soup bowls.

3 ribs celery, cut into ½-inch pieces on the diagonal

4 carrots, peeled and cut into ½-inch pieces on the diagonal

1 large onion, cut into 1-inch pieces

¼ cup heavy cream

3 tablespoons chopped fresh parsley leaves

Emeril's® Essence Creole Seasoning (also referred to as Bayou Blast):

2 ½ tablespoons paprika

2 tablespoons salt

2 tablespoons garlic powder

1 tablespoon black pepper

1 tablespoon onion powder

1 tablespoon cayenne pepper

1 tablespoon dried oregano

1 tablespoon dried thyme

Emeril's® Essence Creole Seasoning (also referred to as Bayou Blast):

Combine all ingredients thoroughly.

SOURCE: "NEW ORLEANS COOKING," BY EMERIL LAGASSE AND JESSIE TIRSCH, PUBLISHED BY WILLIAM AND MORROW, 1993

= CHEF NOTES =

_____

_____

_____

_____

_____

_____

_____

_____

_____

_____

_____

_____

_____

_____

_____

_____

_____

_____

_____

_____

NEW ORLEANS FRIED CATFISH

SERVES 6

Directions

1. Heat oil in a 5- 6-quart Dutch oven (or fryer) until the temperature reaches 350 degrees, making sure to adjust the heat to maintain the temperature.

2. In a shallow dish, big enough for the fish pieces, sift the cornmeal and flour.

3. In a small bowl, combine the Creole seasoning, salt, smoked paprika, and black pepper. Season catfish on both sides with the seasoning mixture.

4. Place buttermilk in a shallow dish. Dip each seasoned fish fillet in the buttermilk, flipping it once to coat both sides. Allow excess buttermilk to drip off and move on to cornmeal mixture. Flip the fillet to coat the other side with cornmeal mixture. Transfer to a wire cooling rack while you repeat the process with remaining fillets.

Oil for frying, about 1 quart

1 cup finely ground cornmeal

1 cup all-purpose flour

2 teaspoons creole seasoning

¼ teaspoon salt

¼ teaspoon smoked paprika

¼ teaspoon black pepper

¼ teaspoon red pepper

¼ teaspoon lemon pepper

6 catfish fillets, rinsed and patted dry

¾ cup buttermilk

continued on next page

5. Gently, add the fillets, 2 at a time, to the hot oil and fry until golden brown, about 6 minutes. Remove the fried fillets to a cooling rack while you fry remaining fillets.

6. Serve immediately.

SOURCE: LAURA FUENTES WITH ADAPTATIONS BY
MRS. GERALDINE WILLIAMS BROOKS

= CHEF NOTES =

LOUISIANA CRAWFISH RAVIOLI WITH CRAWFISH CREAM SAUCE

SERVES 6

¼ cup canola oil

2 cups diced onions

1 cup diced green bell peppers

1 cup diced red bell peppers

2 pounds crawfish tails, peeled and shells reserved

2 tablespoons Creole seasoning

2 tablespoons Tabasco® sauce

5 cups heavy cream, divided

8 eggs, divided

1½ cups chopped green onions, divided

1 cup breadcrumbs

Pre-made pasta sheets or wonton wrappers, as needed

2 cups canned diced tomatoes, with liquid

1 cup sliced shallots

6 cloves garlic

½ cup sherry

4 sprigs fresh thyme

1 bay leaf

Salt and pepper to taste

Directions

1. Heat oil in a large sauté pan over medium-high heat. Add onions and cook until translucent, but with no color, about 5 minutes. Add the peppers, crawfish, Creole seasoning and Tabasco®. Cook until crawfish are cooked through, 1 to 2 minutes, and add 1 cup heavy cream. Reduce until most of the cream has evaporated and pan is almost dry. Remove from heat and allow to cool slightly.

2. Once cool enough to touch, add 4 eggs and 1 cup green onions and mix. Add bread-crumbs gradually and mix to combine. Chill until ready to make ravioli.

3. To make ravioli, roll out a sheet of pasta or use wonton wrappers cut into 3-inch squares. Place a spoonful of the crawfish mixture in the middle of each square. Brush the edges of pasta with remaining egg and fold over to form a triangle. Use a fork to press down the edges and seal. Repeat, using the rest of the filling. Reserve prepared ravioli in refrigerator until ready to cook.

4. To prepare cream sauce, combine remaining 4 cups cream, tomatoes, shallots, garlic, sherry, thyme, bay leaf and crawfish shells in a large sauce pot. Bring to a simmer and cook until reduced by half. Strain into sauce pot and season to taste with salt and pepper. Keep hot.

5. Cook ravioli in boiling salted water until pasta is tender. While pasta is cooking, heat sauce in a large pan. Drain ravioli and add to sauce, simmer for 1 to 2 minutes.

6. Place 10 ravioli on each plate and spoon sauce over top. Garnish with remaining ½ cup green onions.

SOURCE: THE ADVOCATE/LOUISIANA SEAFOOD
PROMOTION AND MARKETING BOARD

= CHEF NOTES =

_____

_____

_____

_____

_____

_____

_____

_____

_____

_____

_____

_____

_____

_____

_____

_____

_____

_____

_____

CHEESY POTATOES WITH SMOKED SAUSAGE

SERVES 6

Directions

1. Preheat oven to 350 degrees. Lightly spray a 13x9-inch baking pan with nonstick cooking spray. Cut sausage into ½-inch cubes. Combine all ingredients in a large bowl.

2. Spread mixture evenly in prepared pan. Bake 40 to 45 minutes or until lightly browned.

3. Let stand 5 minutes before serving.

SOURCE: DELISH.COM WITH ADAPTATIONS BY MRS. GERALDINE WILLIAMS BROOKS

1 package smoked sausage

2 cups shredded Cheddar cheese

1 medium onion

¼ teaspoon ground black pepper

1 bag refrigerated shredded hash brown potatoes

1 cup sour cream

¼ cup butter or margarine

¼ teaspoon garlic powder

= CHEF NOTES =

_____

_____

_____

_____

_____

_____

_____

_____

_____

_____

_____

_____

_____

_____

_____

_____

_____

_____

_____

_____

SMOKED CHILI LIME TURKEY WINGS

SERVES 4 — 2 PER PERSON

Directions

1. In a bowl, mix together the chili powder, white sugar, salt, garlic powder and cayenne pepper.

2. Toss the turkey wing portions in the spice mixture until coated. Place in large plastic zip bags and let seasoning soak in overnight. Set the smoker to 275°F using charcoal and soaked wood chips of choice.

3. Place the turkey wings in the smoker and cook until the internal temperature reaches 170°F, about 2 hours or until tender. Take the wings out of the smoker and squeeze lime juice all over the wings and serve.

Tip: For charcoal grill place wood chips directly on charcoal once charcoal gets hot. For gas grill place wood chips in smoker box.

SOURCE: STEVE CYLKA WITH ADAPTATIONS FROM MRS. GERALDINE WILLIAMS BROOKS & FREDRICK BROOKS JR.

8 turkey wing portions (drums or flats)

1 tablespoon sugar

1 teaspoon black pepper

½ teaspoon cayenne pepper

1 teaspoon onion powder

3 tablespoons chili powder

1 teaspoon salt

1 teaspoon garlic powder

2 limes

1 teaspoon paprika

= CHEF NOTES =

_____

_____

_____

_____

_____

_____

_____

_____

_____

_____

_____

_____

_____

_____

_____

_____

_____

_____

_____

_____

_____

RICE & GRAVY STEAKS

SERVES 3

Directions

1. Pour Worcestershire sauce on steaks and rub it in. Season the meat with 1 tablespoon of Cajun seasoning.

2. Place the ⅓ cup of flour onto a shallow plate. Season the flour with the onion and garlic powders. Dredge each steak in the flour and shake off the excess.

3. Heat the oil in a pan over medium high heat. Once, the oil heats up, add in the steaks. Brown the steaks on each side; about 1 minute per side. When the steaks are browned, place them on a plate and set aside.

4. Add the butter to the same pan and allow it to melt. Once the butter melts, add in the onions and bell peppers. Sauté until the onions begin to brown.

1 pound gravy steaks (sirloin tip, eye of round, chuck, etc.)

1 tablespoon Worcestershire sauce

⅓ cup flour

1 teaspoon onion powder

¼ cup canola oil

1 sliced onion

3 tablespoons flour

Cajun seasoning to taste

1 tablespoon Cajun seasoning

1 teaspoon garlic powder

2 tablespoons butter

½ sliced bell pepper

2 cups beef broth

2 cups cooked, white rice

continued on next page

5. Sprinkle in the 3 tablespoons of flour and stir for 1 minute. Pour in the beef broth while whisking to avoid lumps. Bring the beef broth to a simmer.

6. Sprinkle in the 3 tablespoons of flour and stir for 1 minute. Pour in the beef broth while whisking to avoid lumps. Bring the beef broth to a simmer.

7. Add the steak back into the pan. Reduce the heat to low and cover the pan with a lid. Allow the meat and gravy to smother for about 1 hour or until the steak is tender (be sure to check often to prevent sticking).

8. Taste and adjust seasoning as needed. Serve over warm rice.

Tip: Tony Chachere's or Zatarain's Cajun seasoning works best.

SOURCE: B. COOP

= CHEF NOTES =

AUTHENTIC LOUISIANA CRAWFISH BOIL

SERVES 20

3 pounds yellow onions

6 cloves of garlic

6 lemons, halved

2 whole jalapeño peppers

½ cup salt

1 package (73 ounces) ZATARAIN'S® Crawfish, Shrimp and Crab Boil - Complete

4 pounds small red potatoes

1 sack (35 to 40 pounds) live crawfish, cleaned

1 bunch celery, cut in bite-size pieces

¼ cup ZATARAIN'S® Concentrated Shrimp and Crab Boil

1 box ZATARAIN'S® Crawfish, Shrimp and Crab Boil - In a Bag

12 frozen mini corn-on-the-cob

Directions

1. Fill an 80-quart crawfish boiling pot with a basket ⅓ to ½ with water. Place pot on a jet-style propane burner on high heat. Add salt, onions, garlic, jalapenos and lemon halves (You place onions and garlic in a mesh laundry bag. They usually come in a mesh bag from the grocery store and it can be used as well).

2. Bring to full rolling boil. Stir in Crab Boil Complete. Add potatoes (in their mesh bag from the grocery or a laundry bag). Reduce heat to medium-low. Boil 20 minutes or until potatoes are fork-tender. Remove potatoes.

3. Return water to full rolling boil on high heat. Add crawfish, celery, liquid Crab Boil and Crab Boil bag. Return water to full rolling boil on high heat. Start checking doneness just before water returns to full rolling boil. As soon as small gaps start to appear between the head and the tail on the largest crawfish, they are done. Turn off heat. Add frozen corn and cooked potatoes. Let stand 15 minutes.

Remove corn and potatoes. Let crawfish stand for a minimum of 30 minutes, but 45 minutes is better.

To clean crawfish: Pour live crawfish into a washtub or ice chest; cover with water. Drain. Repeat 3 to 4 times until crawfish are clean. Discard any dead crawfish and debris.

SOURCE: MCCORMICK.COM WITH ADAPTATIONS BY FRED BROOKS JR.

= CHEF NOTES =

_____

_____

_____

_____

_____

_____

_____

_____

_____

_____

_____

_____

_____

_____

_____

_____

_____

_____

_____

_____

_____

_____

SLOW COOKER CRAWFISH & CRAB DIP

SERVES APPROXIMATELY 16

Directions

1. Add all ingredients to slow cooker except seafood and cheese, stir well.

2. Cover and cook on LOW for 6 to 8 hours. Add seafood and cook on HIGH for an additional hour. Add cheese and stir until melted and serve.

SOURCE: NEAL BERTRAND-LAFAYETTE, LA WITH ADAPTATIONS BY FRED BROOKS JR.

1 stick butter, chopped

1 jalapeño pepper, chopped

5 cloves garlic, minced

½ teaspoon dried parsley flakes

12 to 16 ounces real or imitation crabmeat, chopped fine

1 onion, chopped

1 bell pepper, chopped

½ cup green onion tops, chopped

½ cup water

1 pound crawfish tails, peeled, thawed & undrained

1 teaspoon Worcestershire sauce

1 cup cream cheese

Optional: Tabasco® brand pepper sauce to taste

= CHEF NOTES =

_____

_____

_____

_____

_____

_____

_____

_____

_____

_____

_____

_____

_____

_____

_____

_____

_____

_____

_____

_____

SLOW COOKER SPICY CHICKEN WINGS IN BARBECUE SAUCE

APPROXIMATELY 30 WING PIECES

Directions

1. Rinse chicken wings; pat dry. Cut off and discard wing tips then cut each wing at the joint to make two sections. Sprinkle wing pieces with salt, pepper, garlic powder, and onion powder; place wings on a lightly oiled broiler pan.

2. Broil about 4 inches from heat for 10 minutes on each side, or until chicken wings are nicely browned. Transfer chicken wings to slow cooker.

3. In a bowl, combine barbecue sauce, honey, mustard, Worcestershire sauce, and Tabasco®. Pour sauce over chicken wings. Cover and cook on LOW for 4 to 5 hours or on HIGH 2 to 2 ½ hours.

4. Serve directly from slow cooker, keeping temperature on LOW.

SOURCE: NEAL BERTRAND-LAFAYETTE, LA
WITH ADAPTATIONS BY FRED BROOKS JR.

3 pounds chicken wings (16 wings)

Salt & pepper to taste

1½ cups barbecue sauce

Tabasco® to taste, optional

1 teaspoon onion powder

2 teaspoons prepared mustard or spicy mustard

2 teaspoons Worcestershire sauce

¼ cup honey

1 teaspoon garlic powder

=CHEF NOTES=

_____

_____

_____

_____

_____

_____

_____

_____

_____

_____

_____

_____

_____

_____

_____

_____

_____

_____

_____

CAJUN CHICKEN AND FRIED RICE

SERVES 4

Directions

1. Combine rice, water (or broth) and salt in a saucepan. Bring to a boil, then cover, reduce heat to low, and simmer for 14 minutes. Remove from heat and set aside when done. Keep covered.

2. Cut the chicken into bite-sized pieces, about 1-inch cubes. Season generously with Cajun seasoning. Add one tablespoon of the olive oil to a large pot or Dutch oven over medium-high heat. When the oil is very hot, add the chicken in a single layer. Brown on one side, about 2–3 minutes, then flip and brown on the other side. Remove chicken to a plate and set aside.

3. Add the remaining olive oil to the pan, increase heat to high, and when the oil is hot, carefully add the onions and bell peppers. Add more seasoning and cook, stirring occasionally, until the vegetables are softened and browned.

1 cup uncooked rice

2 cups water or chicken broth

1 teaspoon salt

1 pound boneless, skinless chicken breasts

Cajun or Creole seasoning

2 tablespoons olive oil

4 cups diced onions and bell peppers

1 (10-ounce) can Ro-Tel® Diced Tomatoes and Green Chiles

1 cup shredded cheddar cheese

continued on next page

4. Add the tomatoes to the onions and bell peppers, then add the chicken back in, along with any juices that may have collected on the plate. Add the cooked rice and stir until well combined. Add the cheese, if desired, and stir well to combine.

SOURCE: KEVINANDAMANDA.COM

= CHEF NOTES =

_____
_____
_____
_____
_____
_____
_____
_____
_____
_____
_____
_____
_____
_____
_____
_____
_____
_____
_____
_____
_____
_____

THE SWEET STUFF!

CAJUN BLACKBERRY DUMPLINGS

SERVES 4

Directions

1. In a medium mixing bowl, whisk together melted butter, milk, eggs, 1 cup sugar, and vanilla. In a separate bowl, combine flour and baking powder. Add dry ingredients to liquid ingredients and stir, but do not over-mix.

2. When dumpling batter is ready, combine water, 2 ½ cups sugar, and blackberries in a large skillet. Cook fruit over medium heat until mixture thickens. Drop dumpling batter by heaping teaspoonfuls into blackberry sauce mixture in skillet. Cover and cook until dumplings rise.

3. Test them with a fork to see if they are done. When a fork inserted into dumplings comes out clean, remove them from the skillet and continue with the remaining batter.

4 tablespoons melted butter

1 cup whole milk

2 large whole eggs, well beaten

3 ½ cups sugar

2 teaspoons pure vanilla

3 ½ cups all-purpose flour

3 teaspoons baking powder

4 cups bottled water

1 ½ quarts blackberries

Whipped cream or vanilla ice cream for serving

continued on next page

4. Serve warm right out of the skillet with the blackberry sauce mixture ladled over the dumplings. Top each dish with rich dollops of whipped cream or ice cream.

SOURCE: FRANK DAVIS; LOUISIANA COOKING

= CHEF NOTES =

7UP® POUND CAKE

SERVES 12–16

3 cups sugar

3 sticks butter

5 eggs

1 teaspoon lemon extract

3 cups all-purpose flour

¾ cup 7up®

1 teaspoon vanilla extract

Directions

1. Cream butter and sugar until pale. Add eggs one at a time beating well. Blend in lemon and vanilla extract. Blend in flour. Finally, add 7up® and blend well.

2. Bake in bundt cake pan sprayed with cooking spray at 325 degrees for 1 ½ hour or until toothpick comes out clean when stuck in center.

SOURCE: MRS. GERALDINE WILLIAMS BROOKS

= CHEF NOTES =

PRESERVED FIGS

MAKES 7 PINTS OR 14 ½ PINTS

1 gallon (16 cups) firm fresh figs

2 tablespoons baking soda

2 cups water

7–14 fresh cinnamon sticks

7 pint sized canning jars or
    14 ½ pint jars

Boiling water (enough to cover
    figs)

8 cups sugar

Juice of 1 lemon

7 round lemon slices

Directions

1. In a large Dutch oven, combine sugar and 2 cups water and boil briskly for 10 minutes. Lower heat to a simmer and carefully add figs. Simmer uncovered on very low heat until thick and syrupy, for about 1 to 2 hours. Stir only if figs appear to stick to pot and do so very gently.

2. While figs are cooking, sterilize lids and jars for canning: Wash jars, lids, and lid rings in hot soapy water. Boil jars 5 minutes. Boil a few inches of water in a saucepan and remove from heat. Leave jars, lids and lid rings in hot water until ready to use.

3. Add lemon juice to figs during last 10 minutes of cooking. Carefully remove jars from hot water. Add one lemon slice and one cinnamon stick to each jar. Using a slotted spoon, place figs into prepared jars. Ladle syrup over figs until syrup reaches ¼-inch from jar top. Wipe rims with a damp clean paper towel and screw lids onto jars.

4. Process jars in hot water bath for 10 minutes making sure that water is at least 2 inches above jars. Remove jars from water, cool slightly and test for seal.

SOURCE: MRS. GERALDINE WILLIAMS BROOKS

= CHEF NOTES =

_____

_____

_____

_____

_____

_____

_____

_____

_____

_____

_____

_____

_____

_____

_____

_____

_____

_____

_____

_____

VANILLA CUSTARD ICE CREAM

MAKES 1 ½ QUARTS

1 ¼ cups sugar

3 eggs

1 tablespoon cornstarch

1 (12-ounce) can evaporated milk

¼ teaspoon salt

1 cup whipping cream

2 cups milk

4 teaspoons vanilla extract

Directions

1. Stir together sugar, cornstarch and salt. Whisk in milk and place pan over medium heat. Bring to a boil then lower to simmer and cook 1 minute stirring constantly. Remove from heat.

2. Beat eggs well in medium bowl. In a slow stream, whisk in 1 cup of hot milk mixture into eggs. Place in pan with mix over low heat and slowly whisk in egg mixture. Whisk constantly for 2 minutes and remove pan from heat. Strain mixture if lumps have formed.

3. Stir in whipping cream and vanilla extract and chill custard at least 2 hours (preferably overnight). Freeze in ice cream freezer according to manufacturer's directions.

SOURCE: MRS. GERALDINE WILLIAMS BROOKS

= CHEF NOTES =

_____

_____

_____

_____

_____

_____

_____

_____

_____

_____

_____

_____

_____

_____

_____

_____

_____

_____

_____

_____

LEMON POUND CAKE

SERVES 16

Directions

1. Combine all cake ingredients in a large bowl. Beat at high speed for 4 to 5 minutes. Pour into a greased and floured tube pan. Bake for 55 to 60 minutes in a 350-degree oven, or until a toothpick comes out clean. Cool in pan for 15 minutes.

2. If desired, combine ingredients for glaze in a medium sized bowl and drizzle over cake once cooled.

SOURCE: MRS. GERALDINE WILLIAMS BROOKS

1 cup unsalted butter (2 sticks), softened

2 tablespoons fresh lemon juice

4 eggs

1 teaspoon salt

½ teaspoon baking powder

3 tablespoons finely grated lemon zest

2 cups sugar

1 cup buttermilk

3 cups all-purpose flour

½ teaspoon baking soda

½ teaspoon vanilla extract

Glaze:

½ cup fresh lemon juice

½ cup confectioners' sugar

= CHEF NOTES =

SLOW COOKER PEACH COBBLER

SERVES 4 TO 6

Directions

1. Lightly grease slow cooker or spray with non-stick cooking spray.

2. In a large bowl, combine baking mix and sugars. Add eggs and vanilla. Stir.

3. Pour in milk and margarine; stir. Mix in peaches and cinnamon until well mixed.

4. Pour into slow cooker. Cover and cook on low for 6 to 8 hours or on high 3 to 4 hours. Serve warm. Top with vanilla ice cream if desired.

SOURCE: BEST LOVED SLOW COOKER RECIPES BY PUBLICATIONS INTERNATIONAL

¼ cup all-purpose baking mix

½ cup granulated sugar

2 teaspoons vanilla extract

¾ teaspoon ground cinnamon

2 teaspoons margarine or butter, melted

½ cup packed brown sugar

2 eggs

½ can evaporated milk

3 large ripe peaches, billed, pitted, and mashed

Optional: Vanilla ice cream

= CHEF NOTES =

_____

_____

_____

_____

_____

_____

_____

_____

_____

_____

_____

_____

_____

_____

_____

_____

_____

_____

_____

_____

_____

SOUR CREAM CAKE

SERVES 16

Directions

1 cup softened butter

3 cups sugar

6 egg yolks

3 cups flour

¼ teaspoon baking soda

1½ cups sour cream

2 tablespoons almond extract

1 teaspoon vanilla extract

6 egg whites

1. In a large bowl, cream butter and sugar. Add egg yolks one at a time and beat well after each addition. Sift flour three times. Mix baking soda into sour cream.

2. To butter mixture, add flour and sour cream alternately. Add almond and vanilla.

3. Beat egg whites stiff. Fold into batter. Pour into greased, floured tube pan. Bake at 300 degrees for 1½ hours. Cake tester or toothpick should come out clean.

SOURCE: MRS. GERALDINE WILLIAMS BROOKS

= CHEF NOTES =

MAKES APPROXIMATELY 6 DOZEN

2 ½ sticks butter

4 eggs

4 teaspoons baking powder

1 tablespoon milk

¼ teaspoon salt

2 ½ cups sugar

4 cups all-purpose flour

2 teaspoons nutmeg

1 teaspoon vanilla flavor

Directions

1. In a medium bowl, cream together the butter and sugar until smooth. Beat in the eggs one at a time. Stir in the vanilla. Combine the flour, baking soda, salt and nutmeg and sift; stir into the creamed mixture. Knead dough for a few turns on a floured board until smooth. Cover and refrigerate until firm.

2. Preheat the oven to 325 degrees. Lightly flour surface and roll the dough out to ¼-inch in thickness. Cut into desired shapes with cookie cutters. Place cookies 1 ½ inches apart on cookie sheets.

3. Bake for 8 to 10 minutes in the preheated oven. Cool on baking sheet for 5 minutes. Move tea cakes to wire rack to finish cooling

SOURCE: MRS. GERALDINE WILLIAMS BROOKS

= CHEF NOTES =

_____

_____

_____

_____

_____

_____

_____

_____

_____

_____

_____

_____

_____

_____

_____

_____

_____

_____

_____

_____

RAISIN BREAD PUDDING

SERVES 8

Directions

1. Preheat oven to 350 degrees. Grease 12x8 inch baking dish. Combine bread and raisins in large bowl. Combine evaporated milk, eggs, butter, sugar, vanilla extract, cinnamon, and nutmeg in medium bowl.

2. Pour egg mixture over bread mixture and combine well. Pour mixture into prepared baking dish. Let stand for 10 minutes.

3. Bake for 35 to 45 minutes or until center is set.

SOURCE: UNKNOWN

16 slices bread, cubed

1 cup raisins

2 (12-ounce) cans evaporated milk

4 large eggs, slightly beaten

4 tablespoons butter, melted

¾ cup packed brown sugar

2 teaspoons vanilla extract

1 teaspoon ground cinnamon

½ teaspoon ground nutmeg

= CHEF NOTES =

=== 2004 ===
RUM SAUCE

YIELDS 1 ½ CUPS

Directions

1. Cook butter, sugar, and cream in advance in double boiler for 10–15 minutes or until slightly thickened. Refrigerate about 15 minutes before serving.

2. Add remaining ingredients and reheat in double boiler.

SOURCE: MRS. STEPHEN E. PLAUCHE

1 ½ cup butter

½ cup light cream

1 teaspoon vanilla extract

1 cup sugar

Dash of nutmeg

¼ cup (or more) light rum'

= CHEF NOTES =

_____

_____

_____

_____

_____

_____

_____

_____

_____

_____

_____

_____

_____

_____

_____

_____

_____

_____

_____

_____

_____

_____

PEANUT BUTTER COOKIES

MAKES 1 DOZEN

Directions

1. Heat oven to 375 degrees and grease several baking sheets.

2. In a large bowl with electric mixer beat brown sugar, butter and peanut butter until fluffy. Beat in egg and vanilla.

3. Add flour, baking powder and salt. Beat at low speed scraping sides of bowl occasionally until well combined.

4. Shape ¼ cup full of cookie dough into 4-inch round balls and place on green baking sheets leaving 3 inches between cookies. With blunt top edge of large knife press 5 lines evenly spaced across top of cookie dough. Press 5 more in opposite direction to make crisscross effect.

5. Bake cookies for 10 to 12 minutes or until firm and golden. Cool completely on wire rack and store in airtight container.

SOURCE: MRS. GERALDINE WILLIAMS BROOKS

1 cup firmly packed light brown sugar

½ cup chunky peanut butter

2 teaspoons vanilla extract

1 teaspoon baking powder

½ cup (1 stick) butter, softened

1 large egg

½ cup un-sifted all-purpose flour

¼ teaspoon salt

= CHEF NOTES =

_____

_____

_____

_____

_____

_____

_____

_____

_____

_____

_____

_____

_____

_____

_____

_____

_____

_____

_____

CREAMY NO BAKE BANANA PUDDING

SERVES 6

Directions

1. In a large mixing bowl, combine condensed milk, milk, and water. Add pudding and beat until well blended. Chill about 5 minutes. Fold in Cool Whip. Mix well.

2. Line a 2 ½ quart bowl with vanilla wafers.

3. Cover with a layer of sliced bananas, then a layer of pudding. Repeat layering twice, ending with pudding on top. Refrigerate.

SOURCE: D'IDRA T. PLAIN

1 (14-ounce) can sweetened condensed milk

½ cup cold water

4 large bananas, peeled and sliced

1 (16-ounce) container Cool Whip

1 teaspoon vanilla extract

1 cup milk

1 (3.5-ounce) package instant vanilla pudding

1 (16-ounce) bag Jack's® vanilla wafers

= CHEF NOTES =

_____

_____

_____

_____

_____

_____

_____

_____

_____

_____

_____

_____

_____

_____

_____

_____

_____

_____

_____

_____

TRADITIONAL BANANA PUDDING

SERVES 4

Directions

1. Combine sugar, flour, salt, milk, and egg yolks in top of double boiler. Cook stirring constantly, until fairly thick, about 15 minutes. Add vanilla and butter.

2. Layer vanilla wafers and sliced bananas alternately with pudding in 1-quart Pyrex dish. Beat egg whites with a little sugar added to make meringue.

3. Cover pudding with meringue and brown at 400 degrees for about 4 minutes.

SOURCE: MR. WAYNE KEMMERLY JR. &
BILLIE JEAN PRESCOTT

¾ cup sugar

Pinch of salt

1 cup evaporated milk

1 teaspoon vanilla

1 bag vanilla wafers

¼ cup flour

1 cup milk

2 eggs, separated

3 tablespoons butter

2 large bananas, sliced

=CHEF NOTES=

_____

_____

_____

_____

_____

_____

_____

_____

_____

_____

_____

_____

_____

_____

_____

_____

_____

_____

_____

_____

═══ 2008 ═══
ITALIAN CREAM CAKE

APPROXIMATELY 12 SERVINGS

Directions

1. Cream butter and sugar. Add egg yolks one at a time beating after each addition.

2. Stir baking soda into buttermilk. Add sifted flour into batter; alternating with buttermilk mixture. Add vanilla, coconut and nuts.

3. Beat egg white until peaks form and fold into mixture. Pour into greased and floured 9x13-inch cake pan for a sheet cake or three 8- or 9-inch layer pans.

4. Bake in a preheated 325-degree oven for 45 minutes for the sheet cake and 30 to 40 minutes for the layers, or until cake is golden brown. Cool and ice.

Icing:

Beat cream cheese and butter. Add vanilla, confectioners' sugar and nuts. Continue to beat until of spreading consistency.

SOURCE: MARTIE KWASNY

2 sticks butter

5 eggs, separated

1 cup buttermilk

1 teaspoon vanilla

½ cup chopped pecans

2 cups sugar

1 teaspoon baking soda

2 cups flour

1 cup shredded coconut

Icing

1 (8-ounce) package cream cheese, softened

1 teaspoon vanilla extract

½ cup pecans, chopped fine

1 stick butter, softened

1 pound confectioners' sugar

= CHEF NOTES =

_____

_____

_____

_____

_____

_____

_____

_____

_____

_____

_____

_____

_____

_____

_____

_____

_____

_____

_____

_____

_____

NEW ORLEANS BEIGNETS

MAKES 4 DOZEN

Directions

1. In a large bowl, dissolve yeast in warm water. Add milk, oil, sugar, egg and 2 cups flour. Beat until smooth. Stir in enough remaining flour to form a soft dough (dough will be sticky). Do not knead. Cover and refrigerate overnight.

2. Punch dough down. Turn onto a floured surface; roll into a 16x12-inch rectangle. Cut into 2-inch squares.

3. In an electric skillet or deep-fat fryer, heat oil to 375 degrees. Fry squares, a few at a time, until golden brown on both sides. Drain on paper towels. Roll warm beignets in confectioners' sugar.

SOURCE: TASTE OF HOME & BEST OF COUNTRY BREADS

1 package (¼-ounce) active dry yeast

¼ cup warm water (110° to 115°)

1 cup evaporated milk

½ cup canola oil

¼ cup sugar

1 large egg

4 ½ cups self-rising flour

Oil for deep-fat frying

Confectioners' sugar

= CHEF NOTES =

_____

_____

_____

_____

_____

_____

_____

_____

_____

_____

_____

_____

_____

_____

_____

_____

_____

_____

_____

_____

_____

GERALDINE'S PECAN PRALINES

SERVES 20

Directions

1. In a large thick roaster pot or cast-iron pot add sugar and evaporated milk. Mix well and cook over low to medium heat. After mixture begins to thicken, add butter and continue to cook stirring constantly.

2. When mixture reaches about 220 degrees on a candy thermometer, add pecans and continue to cook and stir until mixture reaches the soft ball stage of 240 degrees.

3. Add vanilla and almond extract, remove from heat, and stir briskly. Spoon pralines into 3-inch balls and drop out on foil lined and greased baking sheets (non-stick foil works best and does not require grease). Set baking sheets on racks and allow to cool.

TIP: As mixture thickens you will need to stir more briskly to prevent scorching.

SOURCE: MRS. GERALDINE WILLIAMS BROOKS, FRED BROOKS JR., TONIKA K BROOKS

3 (12-ounce) cans of evaporated milk

3 ½ cups chopped pecans

1 teaspoon almond extract

4 ½ cups sugar

1 ½ sticks of butter

2 tablespoons pure vanilla extract

= CHEF NOTES =

_____

_____

_____

_____

_____

_____

_____

_____

_____

_____

_____

_____

_____

_____

_____

_____

_____

_____

_____

_____

_____

QUICK SWEET POTATO PIE

SERVES 8

Directions

1. Rinse sweet potatoes and bring to a boil. Boil for approximately 45 minutes until done and soft. Rinse sweet potatoes in cold water and peel off skin. Mash sweet potatoes in a large bowl. Add butter and mix well with hand mixer.

2. Mix in eggs, milk, sugar, nutmeg, vanilla, and cinnamon. Beat mixture in large bowl on low to medium speed until well mixed and smooth.

3. Pour mixture into piecrust.

4. Bake on 350 degrees F for about 45 to 50 minutes.

5. A toothpick stuck in center should come out clean when pie is done.

SOURCE: MRS. GERALDINE WILLIAMS BROOKS

2 large sweet potatoes

2 cups sugar

1 stick butter, softened

½ teaspoon ground nutmeg

1 (9-inch) pie crust, unbaked

4 eggs, beaten

1½ teaspoons vanilla flavor

½ teaspoon ground cinnamon

1 teaspoon flour

= CHEF NOTES =

OLD FASHIONED SUGAR COOKIES

YIELDS 5 DOZEN

Directions

1. Cream shortening and sugar. Beat egg and add to mixture. Mix flour, salt and baking powder, and sift together.

2. Add flour mixture alternately with milk and vanilla to the sugar mixture and mix into dough. Roll out and cut.

3. Bake at 375 degrees for approximately 10 minutes.

SOURCE: MRS. DANIEL T. MURCHISON

½ cup shortening

1 egg, beaten

¼ teaspoon salt

½ cup milk

1 cup sugar

3 cups flour

3 teaspoons baking powder

½ teaspoon vanilla

= CHEF NOTES =

_____

_____

_____

_____

_____

_____

_____

_____

_____

_____

_____

_____

_____

_____

_____

_____

_____

_____

_____

_____

_____

_____

_____

CLASSIC PECAN PIE

SERVES 8

1 cup Karo® Light Corn Syrup

1 cup sugar

1 teaspoon pure vanilla extract

1 (9-inch) unbaked deep-dish pie crust

3 eggs

2 tablespoons butter, melted

1½ cups pecans

Directions

Mix corn syrup, eggs, sugar, butter and vanilla using spoon. Stir in pecans. Pour into pie crust. Bake at 350 degrees on center rack of oven for 60 to 70 minutes. Cool for 2 hours before serving.

TIPS: Pie is done when center reaches 200 degrees. Tap center surface of pie lightly—it should spring back when done. For easy clean up, spray pie pan with cooking spray. If pie crust is over browning, cover edges with foil.

High Altitude Adjustments:

Reduce sugar to ⅔ cup and increase butter to 3 tablespoons. Reduce oven temperature to 325 degrees.

*To reduce calories, substitute with Karo® Lite Syrup.

SOURCE: ARGO®, KARO®
AND FLEISCHMANN'S®

=CHEF NOTES=

_____

_____

_____

_____

_____

_____

_____

_____

_____

_____

_____

_____

_____

_____

_____

_____

_____

_____

_____

BLUEBERRY GATEAU

SERVES 6 TO 8

Directions

1. Preheat oven to 350 degrees. Line a 9-inch round cake pan with parchment paper. Grease pan with 2 tablespoons of butter; sprinkle with 2 tablespoons of granulated sugar, turning to coat.

2. In a large bowl, beat remaining ½ cup butter and remaining ¾ cup granulated sugar with a mixer at medium speed until fluffy, 3 to 4 minutes, stopping to scrape sides of bowl. Add egg and almond extract, beating well.

3. In a medium bowl, whisk together flour, baking powder, baking soda, and salt. With mixer on low speed, gradually add flour mixture to butter mixture alternately with buttermilk, beginning and ending with flour mixture, beating just until combined after each addition. Beat in zest. Gently fold in ¼ cup blueberries.

½ cup plus 2 tablespoons unsalted butter, softened and divided

¾ cup, plus 2 tablespoons granulated sugar, divided

1 large egg

¼ teaspoon almond extract

1⅓ cups all-purpose flour

¾ teaspoon baking powder

½ cup whole buttermilk

1¼ cups fresh blueberries, divided

½ teaspoon baking soda

¼ teaspoon kosher salt

1 tablespoon lemon zest

Garnish: confectioners' sugar

continued on next page

4. Spoon batter into prepared pan, smoothing top with an offset spatula. Sprinkle with remaining 1 cup blueberries. Tap pan on counter twice to release air bubbles.

5. Bake 35 to 40 minutes, until a toothpick inserted in center comes out clean. Let cool in pan for 10 minutes. Remove from pan and let cool completely on a wire rack. Garnish with confectioners' sugar, if desired.

SOURCE: LOUISIANA COOKIN'

= CHEF NOTES =

=== 2015 ===
SLOW COOKER APPLE PIE

SERVES 8

8 tart apples, peeled and sliced

¼ teaspoon allspice

¾ cup milk

¾ cup sugar

1 teaspoon vanilla extract

⅓ cup brown sugar

1¼ teaspoons ground cinnamon

¼ teaspoon nutmeg

2 tablespoons butter, softened

2 eggs

1½ cups Bisquick®, divided

3 tablespoons cold butter

Directions

1. Toss apples in large bowl with cinnamon, allspice, and nutmeg. Place in slow cooker. In a bowl, combine milk, softened butter, sugar, eggs, vanilla, and ½ cup Bisquick®. Spoon over apples. Combine 1 cup Bisquick® and brown sugar.

2. Cut the cold butter into mixture until crumbly. Sprinkle this mixture over top of the apple mixture. Cover and cook on LOW 6 to 7 hours or until apples are soft.

SOURCE: NEAL BERTRAND-LAFAYETTE, LA

= CHEF NOTES =

GERMAN SWEET CHOCOLATE CAKE

SERVES 12

1 package (4-ounces) Baker's®
  German's® Sweet Chocolate

¼ teaspoon salt

½ cup water

4 eggs, separated

2 cups flour

1 teaspoon baking soda

1 cup butter, softened

2 cups sugar

1 teaspoon vanilla

1 cup buttermilk

Coconut Filling

1 can (12-ounce) evaporated milk

¾ cup (1½ sticks) butter or
  margarine

1½ teaspoon vanilla

1 package (7 ounces) Bakers
  Angel Flake® Coconut

1½ cups sugar

4 egg yolks, slightly beaten

2 cups chopped pecans

Directions

1. Heat oven to 350 degrees.

2. Cover bottoms of 3 x 9-inch round pans with parchment paper; spray sides with cooking spray. Microwave chocolate and water in large microwaveable bowl on HIGH 1½ to 2 minutes or until chocolate is almost melted, stirring after 1 minute. Stir until chocolate is completely melted.

3. Beat egg whites in small bowl with mixer on high speed until stiff peaks form; set aside. Combine flour, baking soda and salt. Beat butter and sugar in a large bowl with mixer until light and fluffy. Add egg yolks, 1 at a time, beating well after each. Blend in melted chocolate and vanilla. Add flour mixture alternately with buttermilk, beating until well blended after each addition. Add egg whites; stir gently until well blended. Pour into prepared pans.

4. Bake 30 minutes or until toothpick inserted in center comes out clean. Immediately run small spatula around cakes in pans. Cool cakes in pans 15 minutes. Remove from pans to wire racks; cool completely.

5. Prepare Coconut-Pecan Filling and Frosting; spread between cake layers and onto top of cake.

Coconut Filling:

1. Mix milk, sugar, margarine, egg yolks and vanilla in large saucepan. Cook and stir on medium heat about 12 minutes or until thickened and golden brown. Remove from heat.

2. Stir in coconut and pecans. Beat until cool and of spreading consistency.

SOURCE: KRAFT HEINZ WITH ADAPTATIONS BY
MRS. GERALDINE WILLIAMS BROOKS

= CHEF NOTES =

GINGERBREAD

SERVES 10 TO 12

Directions

1. Place eggs, syrup, sugar, and spices in large bowl and beat well. Add dissolved soda.

2. Sift in flour and beat well. Add boiling water and beat lightly and quickly.

3. Place in 9x12-inch pan lined with wax paper. Bake at 325 degrees for 45 minutes.

SOURCE: MR. CHARLES S. WARE, JR.

3 eggs

1 cup sugar

1 teaspoon ginger

2 large teaspoons baking soda, dissolved in ⅛ cup hot water

1 cup dark syrup

1 teaspoon cloves

1 teaspoon cinnamon

2 cups flour

1 cup boiling water

= CHEF NOTES =

_____

_____

_____

_____

_____

_____

_____

_____

_____

_____

_____

_____

_____

_____

_____

_____

_____

_____

_____

_____

_____

OLD FASHIONED PINEAPPLE UPSIDE DOWN CAKE

SERVES 12

Directions

1. Preheat oven to 325 degrees.

2. In a 10-inch heavy skillet with a heat-resistant handle (I use a cast iron skillet), melt ½ cup butter over very low heat. Remove from heat, and sprinkle brown sugar evenly over pan. Arrange pineapple slices to cover bottom of skillet. Distribute cherries around pineapple; set aside.

3. Sift together flour, baking powder, and salt.

4. Separate the eggs into two bowls. In a large bowl, beat egg whites just until soft peaks form. Add granulated sugar gradually, beating well after each addition. Beat until medium-stiff peaks form.

4 eggs

1 cup packed light brown sugar

10 maraschino cherries, halved

1 teaspoon baking powder

1 cup white sugar

1 teaspoon almond extract

½ cup butter

1 (20-ounce) can sliced pineapple

1 cup sifted cake flour

¼ teaspoon salt

1 tablespoon butter, melted

continued on next page

5. In a small bowl, beat egg yolks at high speed until very thick and yellow. With a wire whisk or rubber scraper, using an over-and-under motion, gently fold egg yolks and flour mixture into whites until blended. Fold in 1 tablespoon melted butter or margarine and almond extract. Spread batter evenly over pineapple in skillet.

6. Bake until surface springs back when gently pressed with fingertip and a toothpick inserted in the center comes out clean, about 30 to 35 minutes. Loosen the edges of the cake with table knife. Cool the cake for 5 minutes before inverting onto serving plate.

SOURCE: CATHY-ALL RECIPES

= CHEF NOTES =

_____
_____
_____
_____
_____
_____
_____
_____
_____
_____
_____
_____
_____
_____
_____
_____
_____
_____
_____
_____
_____

Made in the USA
Columbia, SC
15 January 2020